Text copyright © 2007
by Harriet Ziefert Inc.
Illustrations copyright © 2007 by Yukiko Kido
All rights reserved
CIP Data is available.
Published in the United States 2007 by
🍎 Blue Apple Books
515 Valley Street, Maplewood, N.J. 07040
www.blueapplebooks.com
Distributed in the U.S. by Chronicle Books
First Edition
Printed in China

ISBN 13: 978-1-59354-621-2
ISBN 10: 1-59354-621-1

1 3 5 7 9 10 8 6 4 2

stop pop

Yukiko Kido

flip-a

WORD

Word Families

The world is full of print. Written words are everywhere. It's impossible to learn printed words by memorizing them word, by word, by word. To make learning easier, words can be grouped into families.

The words in a word family have two or more letters that are the same. We read "op" words and "un" words, "it" words and "an" words. If you know "op," then it's easier to learn top, pop, and stop.

This book has words from three different word families. All the words in a family rhyme—which means you can add other words to the group by changing the first letter.

It's okay if some of the words you think of are not *real* words. If you make "nop" or "dop" or "zop," it's not wrong— as long as you know the difference between a real word and a nonsense word.

Flip each page and presto-change-o— a new word appears!

The

Family

c
n
k
m
g
p
h
r
d
s
w

top

pop

op on top of pop

stop on top

top cop

The

un

Family

fun

run bun, run

fun to run

fun in the sun

bun run in the sun

The
an
Family

f
l
w
m
g
n
b
r
d
w
t

man

c

f

an fan

man with fan

The op Family

cop	pop
crop	shop
drop	stop
lop	top

The un Family

bun	run
fun	stun
pun	sun

The an Family

ban	man
bran	pan
can	plan
fan	tan

Find the words in each family.

stop man sun
run bun
tan cop
drop shop can top
stun
man plan run can drop
stun
bran lop
pop crop tan
drop stop
fun pan cop man
lop
bun ban shop fun
man plan cop sun
tan bran fan
pun top